DATE DUE

DEMCO 38-297

LEARN THE VALUE OF

Caring

◆

by ELAINE P. GOLEY

Illustrated by Debbie Crocker

◆

ROURKE ENTERPRISES, INC.
VERO BEACH, FL 32964

Library of Congress Cataloging-in-Publication Data

Goley, Elaine P., 1949–
   Learn the value of caring.

   Summary: Presents situations that demonstrate the meaning and importance of caring.
   1. Caring—Juvenile literature. [1. Caring.
2. Conduct of life] I. Title. II. Title: Caring.
BJ1475.G65   1987   179'.9   87-16287
ISBN 0-86592-381-7

Caring

Do you know what **caring** is?

Caring is playing quietly when Mom isn't feeling well.

Caring is keeping the puppy from chewing your brother's slippers.

Giving Grandma a big hug when she comes to
visit shows her you **care.**

Caring is helping your friend climb down a ladder.

Helping your sister with a jigsaw puzzle is **caring.**

When you keep your bicycle clean and shiny,
that's **caring.**

Caring is giving the birds food and water.

You **care** for your cat when you clean her basket.

When you water the flowers you show you **care.**

Putting your toys away before bedtime is **caring.**

Caring is telling Grandma you miss her.

When you help Mom with the housework,
that's **caring.**

Telling your dad you're glad to see him when he comes home from work is **caring**.

23

Caring is drawing pictures with your sister.

When you shovel snow from your neighbor's
sidewalk you're **caring.**

Caring is making your dad his favorite cake
on his birthday.

Caring is thinking about others.

Caring

"Hop into the camper and we'll be on our way," said Mr. Baker.

Mandy Baker; her brother, Jerome; and their mom made sure the campfire was out. Then they all piled into the camper.

"What's our next stop?" asked Mandy.

"Great Mountain Park," said Jerome. "I hope we see some bears!"

It was dark when Mr. Baker pulled into the park campsite.

"Get a good night's sleep," said Mrs. Baker.

Bright and early the next day, Mandy and her mom went for a walk in the woods.

"Yuck! Garbage! What a mess!" said Mandy.

She ran back to the camper and took out her crayons and found some cardboard.

"I'll make a poster. It will remind people to keep the campsites clean," said Mandy. "I can hang the poster on a tree."

How did Mandy's poster show she **cared?**
What would you have done if you were Mandy?

Caring

The day was hot. The hikers were tired.

"This mountain gets steeper with every step," said Sally.

"Someone, please pass me the lemonade," said Jeff. "I'm thirsty."

"Where are the sandwiches?" asked Maria.

Paul opened his bag and passed out the food to his friends. After everyone had eaten, the group rested under some trees.

"Let's walk over to those rocks," Kay said to Mark. "I want to see what is there."

The friends began walking toward the rocks.

"Look at all the pretty flowers," said Kay. "I'm going to pick some."

"Don't," yelled Mark. "They're wild flowers for everyone to enjoy."

How did Mark show he **cared** about people?
How do you show you **care** about people?